BBC MUSIC GUIDES

———

BARTÓK ORCHESTRAL MUSIC

D1433073

BBC MUSIC GUIDES

Bartók Orchestral Music

JOHN McCABE

UNIVERSITY OF WASHINGTON PRESS
SEATTLE

Contents

The music examples are reproduced by kind permission of the following: Boosey & Hawkes Inc. for Ex. 1, 4–6, 7c, 9–26; Editio Musica, Budapest for Ex, 2, 3, 7a, 7b, 8.

First published 1974 by the British Broadcasting Corporation
Copyright © John McCabe 1974
University of Washington Press edition first published 1975
Library of Congress Catalog Card Number 74-19975
ISBN 0-295-95373-x
Printed in England

Introduction

It is often said that Bartók's string quartets, as a group, give the clearest indication of his development as a composer, and to a considerable extent this is true. From the First Quartet (1908) to the Sixth (1939) there is a straight stylistic line, that of the mature, confident Bartók hewing his own personal language out of the various influences at work on him. Even though the First Quartet is a relatively early work, it came sufficiently late in his career for him to have already started the process of assimilating Western concert techniques with the results of the folk-song researches he had commenced some years earlier; so that in this respect, with the mature composer already shaping his own individual style with the utmost conviction, it can hardly be described as anything less than a characteristic work. From this piece, Bartók's development goes through the increasingly experimental style of the Second and Third Quartets, to the achievement of a completely synthesised, absolute mastery in the Fourth, and then the suggestion of emotional expansiveness in the Fifth, to which is added the hint of valediction in the more immediately communicative Sixth.

Each one is thus a satisfying, coherent statement of Bartók's achievements up to the time of writing it. Yet, save for the Fourth (which is surely an expression of stylistic striving), the quartets do not show to any great extent the struggles Bartók underwent to form his own style, nor the experiments he made with the various influences upon him. These appear much more clearly in his orchestral works, which, though as a body far less sustained in inspiration than the quartets, throw much greater light on the processes behind his eventual achievement of complete stylistic synthesis. There is, for instance, nothing in the quartets to reveal as clearly as *Kossuth* the overpowering impact of Richard Strauss's music on the young Bartók, nor anything which reveals the immense influence of Liszt; nor is there a quartet from his last years of self-imposed exile in the USA to compare in relaxed, more accessible vein with the *Concerto for Orchestra* or the Third Piano Concerto; for Bartók's last quartet, with its movingly elegiac, inconsolable tone, predates his departure for America. It is tragic that he did not live to fulfil Ralph Hawkes's commission for a seventh quartet; it would have been fascinating to see whether this sustained the more extrovert mood of the American works or returned to a more introverted, possibly even less optimistic, tone of voice. If the Viola Concerto completed by Tibor Serly is any guide, the Seventh Quartet might well have been closer in spirit to the Sixth than, say, to the *Concerto for Orchestra.*

However, the fact remains that, while the quartets provide a kind of microcosm of Bartók's mature career, his orchestral music often reveals more clearly the sources of his eclecticism and his probing for a technique to unify this. Only one thing is lacking: a major orchestral piece of the same kind, and from the same period, as the great experimental pieces such as the Third Quartet and the Piano Sonata. There are, of course, the piano concertos, but of these only the First really falls into this category (the Second is more relaxed in tone), and otherwise there is only one purely orchestral work from this period, the relatively more accessible *Dance Suite,* hardly an experimental piece. Indeed, it is noticeable that after the *Four Orchestral Pieces* of 1912 Bartók's output of orchestral music was remarkably spasmodic. This may well be attributed to the immense difficulties he encountered in his earliest years with performances of the orchestral works: the Suite No. 1 (1905), for instance, was initially performed only in part, and with almost every major work he experienced great trouble in obtaining performances. It could also be fairly suggested that after 1912 he found he could carry out his experiments more successfully in the fields of piano and chamber music, with their self-contained character and limitations but also their easier potential for performances. In any case, his early orchestral experiments, while often fascinating and illuminating, were only intermittently successful, and it is perhaps significant that possibly his most 'advanced' late orchestral composition without soloist, the *Music for Strings, Percussion and Celesta,* though an example of his mature compositional technique brought to its highest pitch of subtlety and finesse, hardly makes any *technical* move forward, but rather consolidates previous achievements and represents a broadening of his expressive capabilities.

Although his music derived initially from the highly romantic world of Richard Strauss, Liszt, Brahms and Wagner, Bartók was ultimately a classicist, and the increasing classicism of his approach through his career was one feature that enabled him to reach a balance between technique and expression in his last decade or so.

In 1939 he himself said that Bach, Beethoven and Debussy were the three composers from whom he had learnt the most (to which must surely be added the name of Liszt). There is a distinct affinity with the techniques of the late sonatas and quartets of Beethoven (the Op. 131 quartet is an especially illuminating example), while his study of Bach (he published an edition of the '48', among other pedagogical works) must certainly have influenced not only his contrapuntal techniques but also the Baroque vigour of line to be found in so many of his faster movements: one thinks of the first movement of the Second Piano Concerto, with its vital toccata figuration, for example. But equally important, to put it mildly, was the influence of folk-music, derived initially from Liszt's Hungarianism and then from Bartók's discovery of the 'real' Hungarian folk-music. It should be remembered that Liszt's idea of this was the gipsy style and the derivations from the eighteenth-century *verbunkos* (a sergeants' recruiting dance); and while there is a distinction between this and indigenous folk-music, there are close racial and musical links between the gipsies and the ethnic Hungarians, so that close correspondences between the two musics are inevitable.

But Bartók's identification with folk-music went deeper than a mere absorption of superficial expressions of style. Indeed, it is almost impossible to separate those technical methods which he himself derived from concert music and those taken from folk-music. In 1927, in answer to a question from Denijs Dille, he said: 'I place great emphasis on the work of technical arrangement. . . . I do not like to repeat an idea without change, and I do not bring back one single part in exactly the same way. This method arises out of my tendency to vary and transform the theme. . . The extremes of variation, which are so characteristic of our folk-music, are at the same time the expression of my own nature.'[1] This is evident from the start of Bartók's orchestral work, with its Straussian-Lisztian method of thematic transformation. The example of concentrated motivic unity in folk-music, which Bartók found during his researches, simply gave an added impetus to his exploration of a technique already part and parcel of his own manner. Similarly his liking for symmetrical organisation, whether

[1]As quoted in József Ujfalussy: *Béla Bartók* (Corvina Press, Budapest and London, 1971).

on a large scale or in miniature, is as much a personal feature of his own musical inclinations from the outset as it is an aspect of folk-music adopted by him; again, his folk researches must have given him an added impulse to explore this technique.

During this survey of his orchestral music, I hope to show how these, and other aspects of his style and expression, developed and became more and more concentrated. I have adopted a more or less chronological approach to the matter, since by doing so one can more clearly appreciate this development; and one of the most absorbing aspects of this part of his output is the way he explores his techniques, assimilates new influences as he goes, and finally brings all the elements of his style to a peak of unity. As a result, two things should be noted at this stage. First, much of the discussion is fairly technical, because any study of a composer's stylistic development is concerned largely with technical matters, especially when the expression so often arises out of the technical problems with which the composer is dealing. And second, I believe that the works of Bartók's last decade were unequivocally his greatest, not least because he was unable fully to express his deepest, innermost feelings until he had to his own satisfaction achieved complete stylistic synthesis. It has always been fashionable to regard some of the more 'advanced' pieces of the 1920s and 1930s as his finest works, because, being more difficult to approach, it has been presumed that they must therefore be 'purer'. My own views of this will, I hope, emerge as the various works are surveyed. But to accomplish this survey properly a good deal of notice has to be taken of works strictly outside the scope of this booklet. Bartók's orchestral music is often deeply affected by, or related to, his quartets, the opera, the piano music, or the concertos, so that some reference to these works often illuminates some aspect of the orchestral music under discussion. This is especially true of the period between the *Dance Suite* (1923) and the *Music for Strings, Percussion and Celesta* (1936), when some of his most radical developments took place in fields other than orchestral music, with crucial impact on the orchestral works of the last decade.

It is, of course, all too easy to talk about 'style' as if it were something tangible and separate from the essence of the music itself. Robert Simpson has pointed out in his BBC Music Guide to Beethoven's Symphonies that, in this particular case, 'superficial talk about "style" gets us nowhere', because Beethoven's 'style' as evinced in the symphonies was not necessarily a logical, progressive thing but rather a constant, changing redirection of powers and purpose. The same is true, to a certain extent, of Bartók – with one vital difference; for Bartók's stylistic development is an extremely logical, consistent aspect of his music. The relative conservatism of his late works is, in my view, the absolutely inevitable culmination of the trends and directions of his earlier work; and so, in concentrating on the development of techniques and style through his career one reaches a fuller understanding of the significance of the late works in this context. But all the talk about technicalities is irrelevant if the music itself does not speak to the listener with personal character and force. Bartók's music, even at its most intensely withdrawn, does this with an authority that grows throughout his career.

Kossuth

As a child Bartók composed mostly piano pieces and chamber music, and even during his student years at the Budapest Academy of Music it was some time before he tried his hand at a substantial orchestral score. This was the Symphony in E flat, written in 1902-3 not long after he had heard for the first time Richard Strauss's *Also sprach Zarathustra*. Prior to this, the young Bartók had become bogged down by too close an involvement first with Brahms and then with Wagner and Liszt. In his autobiography[1] he referred to the performance he heard of *Zarathustra* as 'like a flash of lightning which whirled me out of this stagnation'. The result was this Symphony. When he played it through on the piano to his mentors, they expressed the fairly unanimous opinion that the Scherzo was the best movement, and it was the only one of which he completed a full score. It is in many ways a curiously Brahmsian piece, but there are also frequent hints of the impact Strauss had made in some characteristically Straussian harmonic side-slips, quite well integrated but with less genuine synthesis of Strauss's chromatic manner and Bartók's more diatonic approach. It is a

[1] 'Selbstbiographie', article in *Musikpädagogische Zeitschrift*, Vienna, 1918; in English, in *Tempo*, London, 1949.

light-hearted, genuinely symphonic piece, in which Bartók's later delight in fugato techniques is significantly foreshadowed and in which there are some subtle rhythmic touches.

The Scherzo was first performed orchestrally in 1904, at the Budapest Academy. The Philharmonic Society, meanwhile, had already given the first performance of *Kossuth* in January, a performance followed a month later by one in Manchester by Richter and the Hallé Orchestra. The difference between *Kossuth* and the Scherzo (which, it should be remembered, was composed only a few months earlier) is quite extraordinary. While the Scherzo is well written formally and instrumentally, in an idiom deriving from Brahms and Strauss, *Kossuth* is a great deal more adventurous in style. Bartók handles the vast romantic orchestra (including quadruple woodwind and eight horns) with absolute assurance and skill. His ability to develop his thematic material has, in the few months between the two works, increased enormously. Above all, he has plunged straight into new problems of composition, rather than relying on past examples, and if *Kossuth* still owes much to senior composers, some of whose influence is still not entirely integrated, it remains an immense leap forward.

Apart from being a reflection of Strauss's influence (seen in the shape of the work as a whole, its quite clear relationship to *Heldenleben* in the concept of a protagonist presented in differing situations, and in many details of technique and atmosphere, not least the intimate tone of the music for Kossuth and his wife), the work demonstrates a new aspect of Bartók's life, namely his profound involvement in the Hungarian nationalist movement. At that time Hungary was still under the Austrian Habsburg yoke. Bartók himself went out of his way to encourage his family to speak and write Hungarian instead of the official German, wore Hungarian national costume, and generally allied himself openly with those elements in Hungarian society calling for liberation. In Kossuth, the nationalist who led the abortive rebellion against Austrian domination in 1848, he found the ideal figure to act as central protagonist in a work which could express this revival of strong national feeling. As the music progresses, indeed, the personalised Straussian treatment of this central figure diminishes, the emphasis shifting gradually to a more epic-national approach, ending with a funeral march which is as much an elegy for Hungary as it is for Kossuth himself.

The work is divided into ten sections, played continuously, from an introductory section depicting Kossuth himself, through a growing sense of anguish (at first expressed intimately by Kossuth himself and his wife and gradually moving on to the national plane), towards the central revolution. To depict the Austrian troops of 1848 Bartók chose to distort quite horrifyingly the *Gott erhalte*, the Austrian national anthem (Haydn's *Emperor's Hymn*) which was also in 1903 the official Hungarian anthem – another source of irritation to the nationalists. His handling of this tune brought forth protests from some Austrian members of the Budapest Orchestra, who refused to play it and stormed out of the rehearsal, thereby creating a good deal of publicity and in the long run doing Bartók's cause no harm at all. A further melodic element in the work is the Rákóczy March, which is closely related to the theme depicting the Hungarian nationalist forces. Otherwise, Bartók's thematic material is original, and considerably more varied in style than in the symphonic Scherzo. Richard Strauss inevitably throws his shadow over some of the invention, not least the theme for Kossuth himself:

Ex. 1
Allegro moderato
[Bassoons, Horns]

But a new element is introduced into Bartók's style, his idea of Hungarian national music. Liszt's Hungarian manner has already been named as a major influence on Bartók's early career, and this makes itself felt for the first time in the orchestral music, to pervasive effect. The Hungarianism is of a decidedly gipsy-like cast; the pentatonic nature of the true folk-music is, generally speaking, absent from this score.

Apart from the influences (of which that of Strauss was rapidly absorbed into Bartók's musical bloodstream, while that of Liszt remained for some time a potent force), there are several indications that Bartók was starting to find his own creative path. The Lisztian type of thematic transformation encouraged him to unify this large form by means of developmental procedures which, though by no means as subtle as in the later works, look forward to his future taut structures. The themes are seldom altered much from one movement to the next, but their development is consistent and satisfying. Indeed, *Kossuth* is a moving and powerful work. Only the battle scene, which has its musical antecedents in Beethoven, Tchaikovsky, and of course *Heldenleben,* fails to integrate properly with the rest of the score. But here one comes up against the fact that propaganda in music is apt to take over control at the expense of musical sense. One wishes that Bartók had invented his own theme for the Austrian troops rather than using one of Haydn's. Had he done so, it must surely have fitted better with the style of the rest of the work, which might well have been something approaching a masterpiece, influences or no. As it is, *Kossuth* remains a curiosity, if a moving one.

The Two Suites

In 1904 Bartók produced arguably his most Lisztian compositions, both for piano and orchestra: the Rhapsody, Op. 1 (a transcription of a piano solo written the same year) and the Scherzo, Op. 2. The latter is modestly titled, for it is in effect a half-hour symphony for piano and orchestra. Indeed, though the solo part bristles with difficulties, it might well be described as a *concertante,* for there are substantial sections in which the argument is orchestral with comments – or nothing at all – from the piano. In this work, that vein of acid humour so personal to Bartók makes a rare early appearance. Both these works continue Bartók's new line of thematic development derived from Lisztian structural methods, while the gipsy-Hungarian influence is still strong, especially in the Rhapsody (a direct descendant of Liszt's *Hungarian Rhapsodies*). The following year, however, he and Kodály began their long friendship and collaboration in folk-song research. Just as *Zarathustra* had been a stroke of lightning across Bartók's musical horizons, so the discovery of indigenous Hungarian music was a new, even more profound illumination. This can be seen quite markedly in the Suite No. 2, the first three movements of which were sketched in 1905 ; but oddly enough the Suite No. 1, Op. 3, written in Vienna in the spring of that year, shows little sign of this impending new direction. Indeed, in some ways it is a retrograde step.

Apart from the piano and orchestra Scherzo, with its concerto style, this Suite is the first of Bartók's near-symphonies to reach full score. He himself said it was of 'symphonic nature', a phrase similar to his description of the later *Concerto for Orchestra*. In its five movements we find the first application of a structure that becomes typically Bartókian, in which a work comprises an irregular number of movements in an overall arch form. The effect is emphasised here by the return, at the end of the finale, to the jolly tune with which the work started, and Bartók places at the centre of the composition an extensive Scherzo, flanked by the two slow movements (a format similar to that used in the tripartite middle movement of the Second Piano Concerto). A new development is the extent to which Bartók relates the themes of the movements in an attempt to unify the whole work. This is done fairly simply, with straightforward and seldom subtle relationships; in Ex. 2, for instance, the similarity between the very opening theme (a), the main tune of the central Scherzo (b) and the first subject of the fourth movement is obvious:

More indicative of some future aspects of Bartók's mature music is the flourish which begins the finale (Ex. 3); similar rising phrases, coming to a pause on the top note, occur in many of his later works. And the theme which follows this, with its disruption of the basic E major tonality by the use of an A sharp (the augmented fourth) on the beat, and its alternation of 2/4 and 3/4 metres, is utterly characteristic:

But these are almost all the indications of the later Bartók to be found in the First Suite, save for a few moments of typically fantastic humour and, in the second movement, an atmospheric passage which anticipates the forest music in *The Wooden Prince*. Even Brahms, whose shadow has long been absent from Bartók's music, is vividly recalled here and there in the first movement by some flowing thirds and sixths; Strauss and Liszt are strongly in evidence from time to time, while the Scherzo has all the *élan* – and the manner – of a Dvořák Slavonic Dance. Even the Overture to *Prince Igor* is echoed in the finale. By themselves, these influences mean little. But it is significant that, in this his largest work so far, Bartók relied more heavily than for some time on past example, and also that his orchestral technique is less assured, less varied, than in previous pieces. There are patches of inspired sonority, some attractive solo writing, and some invigorating *tutti*s, but he relies far too much on the full weight of the *tutti* to drive the music forward and provide its impact. He seems strangely reluctant to explore that area between the *tutti* and the lightly accompanied solo, potentially so rich for exploration, so that though there are many touches one would not wish to be without (the expressively gipsy-like cor anglais meditation at the start of the second movement, for instance) the work as a whole never really gets off the ground. Formally, each movement is self-contained and satisfying; in the long run the work advances his mastery of the large form while marking a recession in his purely orchestral technique.

In the Second Suite, however, both form and orchestration show a significant advance, and his folk-song researches make their effect felt. It is odd that the earlier pieces, with their Liszt-Erkel type of Hungarianism, had been well received, while the Second Suite, which for the first time manifests the spirit of genuine Hungarian folk-song, should have been viewed with greater hostility. This is even more curious when one realises that it is only in the finale that this new element makes its unambiguous appearance; the rest still derives basically from the traditions in which Bartók had already been working. But there are considerable differences between this work and its predecessor, even though most of the Second Suite was written along with the First (the finale was delayed until 1907, and it should be pointed out that Bartók revised the work in 1920 and 1943). It is significant that his original title was *Serenade,* and the smaller orchestra used here, against the array employed in the First Suite, bears out the more relaxed nature of the ideas. Yet it is far more resourceful instrumentally; using smaller forces, and working on a more modest scale, Bartók seems able to explore more imaginatively the possibilities for sound coloration offered by the symphony orchestra. The evocation of the sound of a cimbalom towards the end of the second movement is one of the most imaginative effects in his orchestral music to this date; and in exploring the full range of orchestral techniques, from orchestral *tutti*s (which in this more varied context make more impact) to chamber-like delicacy, he shows his increasing self-confidence. Even at the very start of the work, the harp setting the scene (just as in the Second Violin Concerto, twenty-odd years later), solo cello announcing the main theme (Ex. 4) and then an answer to this in divided violas – all this bespeaks a new Bartók with an infinitely richer range of resources at his command.

Ex. 4
Comodo
[Cellos]

p molto espressivo

This theme has a new fluidity, both melodic and rhythmical, and the rising fourths in the third bar demonstrate the growing importance of this interval to Bartók. There is a clear relationship with the preponderance of fourths in folk music; even though his folksong work had hardly begun, his mind had begun to use this interval quite naturally. There is some intermittent Straussian chromaticism during the work, but the predominant feeling is quite different from that of any of Bartók's previous orchestral works, and much more personal. There are even several strong suggestions of the *Concerto for Orchestra,* to be written nearly forty years later. For all the influences, Bartók is beginning to find his own distinctive voice: the process of assimilation has begun. Only in the finale is there any sense of stylistic dichotomy; the main theme (Ex. 5) brings the world of the Hungarian plains into the concert hall with immense effect:

but it is made to exist cheek by jowl with some intensely chromatic material, so that one is not surprised when the movement seems almost to fall apart at the seams and disperse itself towards the end, though the close itself is lovely.

Despite the uncertainty of aim in the finale, however, the work as a whole is delightfully imaginative. In the second movement (*Allegro diabolico* in the two-piano version of 1941) Bartók anticipates his pounding, demonic scherzi of the future. Here, though there is much life in the pulsating accompaniments and the brilliant appoggiaturas, the music is hardly as diabolic or barbarous as this particular genre was to become, but it does have a vital forward impetus. Bartók's growing contrapuntal freedom, evinced throughout the Suite, comes to the fore in a lengthy fugal section demonstrating the change from a predominantly harmonically inspired counterpoint (after Strauss) to a newly concentrated linearity of impulse. The fugue also shows his new command of the plasticity of the material, for the subject itself is altered from time to time, both rhythmically and melodically. His sense of grotesque humour, already in evidence in earlier pieces, is shown in this movement, notably at the end, when Bartók introduces a solo violin parody of the fugue subject, followed by fragmented little phrases thrown about from one instrument to another before the movement ends with a series of shrieks from the full orchestra. It is an altogether unexpected ending, and an oddly disturbing one.

Equally striking is the third movement (*Scena della puszta*), a moving, spacious evocation of the Hungarian plains. This has no symphonic aspirations, nor any epic historical pictorialism, just a simple folk mood, which is achieved by a long opening bass clarinet solo unfolding a freely expressive span of melody. When this theme returns it is more fully scored for cor anglais, clarinets and bassoons, with a surrounding tracery of harps, tremolo violins, and woodwind trills creating an extraordinary feeling of spacious natural beauty. Even the heightened intensity of the more richly chromatic section which precedes this cannot disturb the stylistic equilibrium of the movement as a whole. In the finale, as already suggested, there is an imbalance between the main theme's simple diatonicism and the almost atonal nature of some of the other material, yet at the end of the work, with the folk-song seeming to die away into the distance, criticism is swept away. There is a lovely passage before the end which I cannot resist quoting, in which Bartók combines the gently pulsating accompaniment, the the main tune (cellos and basses), and its answer (flutes and oboes), at a much slower tempo, culminating in a chord (marked *x*) which adds a touch of delicious chromaticism:

The sense of regret suggested by the introduction of this chromatic chord in such a diatonic context is poignant. It can almost be seen, technically, as a farewell to Strauss and Wagner, but the effect is that of personal reaction to something beautiful which is vanishing for ever, a magnificent sunset, perhaps, or the shades of autumn. There is a touch of pastoral innocence about even so sophisticated a device, and this, above all, is the feeling the work gives: its translucent charm is irresistible.

But its superficial charm should not mislead one into regarding it purely as a picturesque piece, for it marks a definite advance in Bartók's handling of both motivic development and tonality. There is nothing very startling about these; they are still clearly derived from traditional procedures. But already he shows his liking for motivic treatment of his material. In the first movement, which is a kind of sonata form with a double exposition, the development is based almost entirely on a subsidiary figure which occurred in passing in the exposition without appearing in any way significant, a truly Haydnesque device. The two expositions themselves show from the start this new freedom of tonality, too. They both pursue the same course – statement of theme (Ex. 4), answer and development – to some degree of intensity, but each time there is a quite distinct tonal shift. The first exposition starts firmly in B flat major and ends with a pause in D major; the second starts firmly in B flat major again, and ends with a pause on G major. Even the processes for the recapitulation (which is interwoven with the development) and the codas are unusual, with a good deal of D flat major interrupting the harmonic scheme of things, until at last a series of chromatically designed chords leads back, with a final twist, to the tonic B flat major. Of all the movements in the Second Suite, it is the first which extends Bartók's technique in these respects, and the frequent pauses in the music (the episodic nature of which thus demands this new degree of motival unity to bind it together again) mark a further stage in his absorption of folk-music influences.

Portraits and Pictures

After the revelation of the new Bartók afforded by the Second Suite it is interesting to note how in his following works he evaded some of its folk-song implications. In 1907 he brought forth several sets of folk-song arrangements for various forces, and in 1908–9 worked on the folk-based series of piano pieces *For Children*. The *Ten Easy Pieces* (1908) also contain a number of folk elements; he returned to this set in the 1930s in his set of *Hungarian Sketches* for orchestra (see page 45). But his larger works are far more 'advanced' in style, and they extend the chromatic implications of his earlier pieces. In the First Violin Concerto (1907–8), the *Two Portraits,* Op. 5, begun in 1907, the *14 Bagatelles* for piano (1908), the First String Quartet (1908, and the most masterly of this group of works of this period), and the *Two Elegies* for piano (1908–9) Bartók moves towards an expressionist handling of chromaticism. There are frequent passages in them which inhabit something approaching the world of Schoenberg's *Verklärte Nacht* or First Chamber Symphony, sometimes with even more rigorous intensity (the use of piled-up fourths in one of the piano *Bagatelles* exceeds in its thoroughness anything in the First Chamber Symphony, for instance), while his new interest in the thematic use of major-minor thirds, hinted at in the Second Suite, becomes a more important element in his style. This last feature has personal connotations linking the First Violin Concerto, the *Bagatelles* and the *Portraits* together, for at the time of composition Bartók had a close relationship with a young violinist, seven years his junior, Stefi Geyer. It was to her that Bartók, in his letters, poured out the most open statements of his religious beliefs and humanitarian views; her devout beliefs and his atheism (a rejection of his early Catholicism, up to the age of fourteen) made an irrevocable split between them inevitable, but before that he wrote his First Violin Concerto for her. It is scarcely surprising that, in view of the intensity of their relationship and the ultimate parting as well as the growing complexity of his music, the works of this period should be far removed in spirit from the simplicity of folk-music and should inhabit a more expressionistic world; to this the influence of Debussy gave an added richness.

Stefi Geyer herself is personified by a theme which closely links these three works. Bartók himself wrote the motif out in a letter to her, writing above it, 'This is your *leitmotiv*', giving it the form in Ex. 7a overleaf. It appears more or less thus in the thirteenth of the piano *Bagatelles,* entitled 'Elle est morte. . .' ('She is dead. . .'); the last of the *Bagatelles* ('Ma mie qui danse. . .' – 'My lover who is dancing. . .') is a truly Lisztian (or Berliozian) metamorphosis of this *idée fixe* into a demonic waltz (Ex. 7b). In the First Violin Concerto, a two-movement work, the first movement derives from an intense contrapuntal treatment of a theme using the same motif as its starting point (Ex. 7c).

The *Two Portraits* combine the other works of this Stefi Geyer triptych. The first, entitled *The Ideal,* is simply the first movement of the Violin Concerto, while the second, *The Grotesque,* is an orchestral version of the last *Bagatelle* given a fresh title. It is

significant that according to Denijs Dille, as quoted by Ujfalussy, it was early in 1908 that Stefi Geyer brought her close relationship with Bartók to an end; the bitterness behind *The Grotesque* and the last two *Bagatelles* surely reflects his feelings about this. In the *Portraits* the juxtaposition of the warm emotion of the first movement and the bitterness of the second makes a moving emotional contrast: two sides of the coin presented with a good degree of spiritual balance.

The idea of paired movements is something already seen in the Second Suite and is a notable formal device throughout Bartók's career; the *lassú* and *friss* of Hungarian folk-music (slow and fast respectively), in fact. But in the *Portraits* the scheme is not carried through with a structural balance to match its emotional interdependence. The first movement, a mere fourteen pages of score, is a fully worked-out piece, slowly unfolding its serenely beautiful polyphony to an intense climax with an almost Bergian luminosity, and ending with heart-rending radiance. The second is a grotesque scherzo, imbued with a spirit of acid, bitter parody but much too short to act as a genuinely structural counterbalance to the larger scope of the first movement, with its expansive flow of music.

Bartók's next orchestral work, the *Two Pictures* (sometimes known by its French title, *Images*), marks significantly the impact of Debussy's music, notably in the first movement with its whole-tone colouring. This is not an entirely unforeseen development, for the influence of the tritone has already been noted as a prominent feature of Bartók's style (see Ex. 3, for instance), and this is an essential part of the whole-tone scale. But here, in the first Picture, the tritone pervades the material to a much greater extent, not only in passing references to Debussyan whole-tone scales but also in melodic inflections and harmonic implications. It does not, so far, affect the tonality (in the way that, say, the first movement of the *Music for Strings, Percussion and Celesta* is a progression from A to E flat and back again), but this more deeply pervasive use of it is new, and it is an integral part of the second Picture, a *Village Dance* in Bartók's beloved festive duple metre:

Ex. 8

The *Pictures* are not so closely related to each other as are the *Portraits*; the use of the first Picture's main theme in the second is not as strong a unifying force as the *leitmotiv* in the earlier work. But they are extremely interesting pieces, not least for the lusciously impressionistic orchestral style of the first, *In Full Bloom*. It is used to express a mood of sombre and intense gloom, clearly anticipating *Bluebeard's Castle,* written the following year (1911). Bartók's characteristic metrical fluidity is present in the ease with which he varies the bar-lengths. In the *Village Dance* one notes the tendency of melodic phrases to curl in chromatically on themselves (another mature characteristic) and also the placing of the dissonant chords, which with their major-minor ambiguity are typically Bartókian. Above all, perhaps, the work is most significant for the fixing of the Lydian mode, of which the tritone is such an essential component, as a central point of his style.

Rumanian Dance

It would be more correct to describe the folk element in the *Village Dance* as Rumanian rather than Hungarian in style, and Bartók's next orchestral piece, in 1911, was in fact his orchestration of the first of the two *Rumanian Dances* for piano, composed the previous year. Technically speaking, these properly belong with the group of suites of folk-based pieces of a light character, mostly compiled from earlier material in the 1930s and dealt with later (see pages 44–6), but this particular piece is exceptional in being scored for a larger orchestra and considerably more substantial in scale. It is worth recalling Bartók's own division of his folk-based works into different categories. Writing to the Rumanian folklorist Octavian Beu in 1931 in connection with those works of specifically Rumanian origin, he suggested this arrangement of categories:

'1a.   Arrangement of Rumanian folk-melodies. . .

1b.   Works in part utilising Rumanian folk-melodies. . .

2a.   Works with original thematic material, but of a completely Rumanian character. . .

2b.   Works with original thematic material, partly of Rumanian character. . .

3.   Setting to music of Rumanian texts. . .'

He himself placed the *Rumanian Dance* in category 2a; as example of the other divisions he cited such works as the popular *Rumanian Folk Dances* (1a), the violin Rhapsodies (1b), part of the third movement of the *Dance Suite* (2b), and the *Cantata Profana* (3).

This Dance is in ternary form, the main theme announced straightaway by solo bassoon with a quiet timpani accompaniment. (There is a real anticipation here of the start of the bassoon theme at the opening of the later *Dance Suite*.)

These first eight bars are repeated, followed by a bar in which the accompaniment moves to an E flat basis, and then the bassoon inverts the theme (Ex. 9b). After some development of this material, especially the motif *x*, a third version of the theme is heard on cellos (9c). Curiously enough, there is no conventionally built climax before the middle section appears; the music rather concerns itself with a quick, but slightly casual, investigation of the material stated thus far and coming almost to a full stop before the *Lento* is ushered in by the violins (9d). This new theme is a further development of Ex. 9a, however, given a totally different sound by the richly evocative, pulsating, swirling accompaniment which partners each phrase, and by the expansion of the tritonal implications of 9a to give the music a more prominently whole-tone flavour. The recapitulation of the fast section, in which Ex. 9c is merely hinted at and which Ex. 9a dominates, reaches the climax deferred from the first part, and after some rumination on the original theme there is a powerful conclusion.

Slight though it is, the *Rumanian Dance* marks a distinct advance in Bartók's concentrated handling of his motivic material, with inversion, expansion of intervals (the fourths of Ex. 9c against the thirds of 9a and 9b) and the extensive *parlando* treatment and change of intervallic emphasis shown in Ex. 9d. There is also the distinctly improvisatory feeling of the *Lento*. Here, as in much of the Second Suite, one senses a kinship with the bardic freedom of folk-song. His handling of tonality, however, is quite different; there are many pedal points and ostinati, the music hardly moving significantly from its C minor tonic basis. The work is impelled forward by rhythm and motivic development; even contrapuntal treatment is largely absent.

'Bluebeard' and the Four Pieces

In the same year as the orchestral *Rumanian Dance*, Bartók completed his only opera, the one-act *Bluebeard's Castle*. Though, strictly speaking, outside the scope of this survey as far as any detailed consideration goes, this work does clearly impinge on the composer's orchestral development, and it is spiritually a crucial point in his career. The close motivic unity which was becoming such an essential part of his technique gives the score a musical intensity to match its emotional tautness. Both Bartók and his librettist Béla Balázs derived much of their inspiration from ancient Hungarian folk-ballads, the mood of which is certainly a major factor in the opera. So too is Bartók's adoption for the vocal lines of a semi-declamatory manner, which derives as much from the close relationship between national speech-rhythm and the musical metre of Eastern European folk-music as it does from the example of Debussy's highly developed continuous recitative in *Pelléas et Mélisande*, an opera which certainly influenced Bartók in this work. The scoring, for massive orchestra including organ, remains one of his most astonishing achievements (only the *Miraculous Mandarin* exceeds this wizardry); the Lake of Tears, for instance, is evoked with an incredibly emotive, highly intricate texture.

It seems likely that Bartók's own solitary nature attracted him to this subject, the opera ultimately turning on Bluebeard's tragic isolation. Yet there does seem to be something almost decadent about an opera concerned largely with the ultimate refusal of a sick neurotic man to achieve a lasting relationship with a woman, a decadence emphasised by the rather self-indulgent way the libretto smacks its lips over the glittering jewels, the gorgeous flowers, and above all the all-permeating blood. Bartók's score admittedly refrains from echoing this excess of lusciousness (one dreads to think what Schoenberg in his early days would have made of it); only a few moments of past-*Parsifal* perfume suggest this tendency. But, though the characters seem drawn with rare clarity and conviction, the element of decadence vitiates the final structure of the opera. Bluebeard does not gain one's sympathy as Peter Grimes does; nor, to take a composer nearer to Bartók, is there the more human warmth and supreme acceptance of fate that makes Maurya in Vaughan Williams's *Riders to the Sea* such a noble operatic figure. This failure at the centre of *Bluebeard's Castle* is emphasised by the fact that it is the more sympathetic Judith on whom the dramatic prominence is placed at the start; Bluebeard himself only gradually takes over the dominating role, and by then it is perhaps too late to have established him as a character who gains our sympathy.

The importance of this aspect of the opera is considerable. We know Bartók to have been an introverted, basically lonely person, despite his deep family involvement. It could so easily have happened that his music would follow the spiritual, and ultimately sterile, path suggested by Bluebeard. In the long run, especially after the Fourth Quartet's final struggles for complete stylistic synthesis, his range of expression broadened; the loneliness of the later works is that not of rejection but of human pity and compassion. But it is surely significant that the *Four Orchestral Pieces,* Op. 12, written in 1912, the year after *Bluebeard,* is one of his least successful works; though it marks a further step forward in some technical respects, its expression is confused. The first movement, *Preludio,* inhabits a world not unlike the flower garden of the first of the *Two Pictures* (though with more exotic blooms) tinged with the bitterness of Bluebeard's Lake of Tears. The following *Scherzo* is far more savagely biting than any of Bartók's previous orchestral movements of this kind, anticipating at times the violent street music of *The Miraculous Mandarin.* In the *Intermezzo,* a gentler, siciliano-like waltz, the music is suffused with a remote, Holstian radiance, while the finale, a *Marcia funebre,* reverts to the epic, tragic style of the end of *Kossuth,* with a deeper underlying bitterness. There are moments in this work when Bartók approaches as near as he ever did to the atonality of Schoenberg, and it is worth recalling that the previous years had seen the completion of Schoenberg's *Five Orchestral Pieces* and Webern's set of six, though the Bartók work is nearer to a genuine symphony than these. But it is the strange mixture of styles and the apparent lack of spiritual aim that make it such an unsatisfying work. There are advances in his handling of tonality on a large scale, in his orchestral technique (he adds a piano to the armoury, using it with much imagination), and in the interesting foretastes of works to come; but the spirit behind the music seems confused. It is as if Bartók felt that the spiritual way of *Bluebeard* was not the one he should take, but could not yet find the way out of its negative properties. Oddly enough, the *Four Pieces* were not orchestrated until 1921, by which time Bartók had begun to find his way out of the morass his orchestral music had got itself into; the works which enabled him to do this were the two widely contrasting ballets.

The Ballets

It was not until 1916 that Bartók completed another work for full orchestra, *The Wooden Prince,* on which he started in 1914. The intervening years – during which the First World War raged – saw the composition of a large number of folk-based works, including the little Piano Sonatina. *The Wooden Prince* is called a 'pantomime' rather than a ballet, and Balázs once again provided the scenario, in which the scene is set in an enchanted countryside containing two castles. The Prince, who lives in one, falls in love with the Princess next door, but his attempts to reach her are thwarted by the Fairy, who enchants the intervening forest so that first the trees and then the waters of the river rise to bar his way. When eventually he does win through, the Princess pays no attention to him until he devises a makeshift puppet out of wood, putting his cloak around it and crowning it with his own hair and crown. The Princess descends and dances with the puppet. Then the Fairy, for no apparent reason, decides to intervene once more and reverse the roles, giving back to the Prince his hair, cloak and crown; the Princess decides that she is no longer interested in the puppet and desires the real Prince, but he rather petulantly spurns her. The forest rises again, this time to bar *her* way, and she desperately throws off her cloak and cuts off her hair. At the end the two are reconciled.

There are obvious problems in the setting of a story which for much of its time is a repetition of previous events arrived at by an incomprehensible change of mind on the part of one of the characters, and in the last third of the ballet score Bartók loses his way a little, writing a good deal of resourceful but ultimately unmemorable 'stage business' music. But even here there is some fine invention, and fortunately in 1931 he made a Suite, which preserves in concert form many, though not all, of the work's best ideas. In this form the score reverses the order of some of the events (the episode of the Prince with the puppet is now placed before the *Dance of the River* instead of after it), and it encompasses the narrative only up to the *Dance of the Princess with the puppet.* From here it omits the events attendant on the Fairy's change of mind and jumps to the ballet's peaceful, brief conclusion. There are one or two slightly awkward joins in the Suite, but it is an immensely enjoyable piece despite the omission of much attractive material, and its neglect in the concert hall is surprising. The sections retained in the Suite give a clear idea of the range of styles in the ballet—not always, it must be said, to its own advantage; for the contrast between the lusciously impressionistic nature music of the trees and the river, the folk-like themes accorded to the Prince and Princess, the more grotesque, biting music characterising the puppet, and the intensely emotional phrases which convey the reactions of the characters to the events involve wide fluctuations of style.

But to regard this as a reason for simply dismissing the work as a failure is, in my view, futile. The start of the Suite gives us a lengthy build-up on a C major chord, strongly coloured by the introduction of an F sharp (the augmented fourth once again), scored with growing majesty and strength. The *Dance of the Princess* which follows, showing her at play alone in the forest, characterises her by means of a lyrical clarinet theme:

The lightness of scoring here contrasts with the increasing richness and power of the following *Dance of the Trees*. The swirling textures, constantly thickening and becoming weightier, provide a background for the Prince's struggles to reach the Princess, his efforts depicted by a strongly scored chordal theme, rhythmically marked by the essential Magyar 'Scotch snap': ♫ . The scene between the Prince and the puppet contains the closest combination of stylistic elements in the work, with the puppet's growing life depicted by themes initially of strong folk character, scored with percussive sharpness, but increasingly of grotesque emphasis. With a sudden change of texture to glittering luminosity the Suite switches to the *Dance of the River*, in which a flowing, express-ive melody in the middle register (coloured by the use of a saxo-phone) is surrounded by a full, flowing tracery of sound. The textures become ever more elaborate until an *agitato* climax leads us to the *Dance of the Princess with the puppet*. Here again the music is at first strongly folk-influenced; the pounding, village-dance character of Ex. 11 shows this:

There is a clear relationship here between this music and so many of Bartók's duple-metre dance movements. It gradually disperses to lead us to the *Postlude* and a return to the original C major, coloured as at the beginning by the tritonal implications of the F sharp and by the scoring, in which horn lines against a soft, velvety background create a memorably haunting atmosphere. The *Postlude,* in the ballet as in the Suite, emphasises once more Bartók's delight in the sense of an arch-form, less rigorously pursued here than in other works, but still a potent force.

It is in the nature music at the beginning and the end, with its uncanny evocation of a vast green forest, and in the music for the trees and the river, that Bartók conjures up more vividly than before a direct image of nature. His deep love of nature was to provide some of the most remarkable passages in his later works, from the point of view of sheer texture: here, for the first time, he applies the lessons of his impressionistic phase, and the influence of Debussy in particular, to a direct evocation of nature. The weirdly distorted music for the puppet and the invigorating folk-dance passages are both supremely well realised. Only the juxtaposition, often quite stark, of these various styles results in the disparity that prevents the work from achieving a sense of complete unity. But even so, and even if it is a lesser work, its charm and fascination are captivating.

THE MIRACULOUS MANDARIN

From 1916 to 1918 Bartók produced an immense number of short works and sets of pieces. His tendency in this direction was prompted to some extent by his folk-song researches, which in 1913 had spread to North Africa; the scherzo of the Second Quartet, written in 1915–17 and thus overlapping with the composition of *The Wooden Prince,* is based on a pounding theme of distinctly Arabic intonation. His concern for integrating the main elements of folk-music with his own style also played a part in this output, which ranged from straightforward folk-song arrangements to the Piano Suite, Op. 14, the much more advanced *Studies,* Op. 18, in which he once more revived the spirit of Liszt's virtuoso pianism while venturing on to the borders of atonality, and of course the Second Quartet. In its sheer concentration of thought and its lack of emotional excess, this quartet surely represents the high point of his career so far, at any rate in terms of stylistic integration; all the diverse elements that make up his style have at last become a complete, indivisible unit. Even the Berber inflections of the Scherzo are inseparable from the material of the rest of the work.

When, in 1918–19, he came to write his third, and last, stage work, *The Miraculous Mandarin,* he was thus fully in command of his stylistic resources. From now on there were to be no more culs-de-sac like the *Four Orchestral Pieces,* no new influences to set him off in a completely new direction, and no wild stylistic discrepancies within a single work. In the next decade or so, his deepest concern technically was to be his intense compositional technique within his now established stylistic format. His personal reaction to the political upheavals surrounding him, expressed in terms of ultimate hopelessness in the Second Quartet, was possibly what impelled him towards a new dramatic subject of quite exceptional horror in the *Mandarin.* The narrative concerns a girl forced by three thugs to stand in a window overlooking the street and lure men in, to be robbed of their money. The first two victims are both penniless, an elderly rake and a timid youth, who are thrown out into the street again. Then an eerie figure is seen in the street and heard coming up the stairs; it is the Mandarin. The girl is at first reluctant to dance before him, but his apparent impassivity forces her, once she has started, to become increasingly passionate. Suddenly he grabs her, she struggles with him and escapes from his embrace, and there ensues a wild dance of pursuit. Eventually he catches her, but now the three thugs leap out of their hiding place, rob him of his valuables and try to kill him. They smother him under cushions, stab him with a sword, and then hang him, but each time to no avail; his eyes are fixed passionately on the girl. Only when they cut him down from the rope and the girl embraces him of her own free will can his wounds begin to bleed, and he dies.

Strong stuff indeed, and this proves to be arguably the most astonishing orchestral score of Bartók's career. Towards the end of the ballet, when the Mandarin is cut down after being hanged and begins to glow with a greenish-blue light, Bartók uses a wordless, off-stage chorus to enhance textures already full of primeval horror; but this section has been omitted from the Suite made in 1919, which ends at the climax of the Mandarin's pursuit of the girl, while she is struggling with him, and before the thugs leap out. Up to this point, with one short cut, the Suite is the same as the ballet score; only the last few bars have been changed to make a proper concert ending. Thus the most horrifying of all the ballet's sections have been omitted. But even the ballet as a whole, despite the more 'illustrative', episodic nature of the final sections, makes a more coherent impression than *The Wooden Prince,* because it is imbued with the utmost thematic unity, a tautness that keeps the essential line through the music even when it is apparently disjunct, and there are none of the changes of style that mark the earlier work.

Restricting ourselves solely to the Suite, we can see an overall shape that divides itself into more or less distinct units. There is a Prelude, depicting the noises of the busy street outside, with car-horns and general bustle. The curtain rises, the three vagrants enter and, having discovered that they have no money themselves, force the girl to the window to lure in victims. This process gradually winds the music down for the start of the second section, in which the girl performs her first 'decoy game' (the score's description). The old rake enters, and he and the girl dance until, at the peak of the intensity, the thugs rush in and throw him out. The music rushes down to a standstill again, and the third section begins. This pursues the same dramatic course; the decoy game, entry of the timid young man, dance (with a rise in intensity), and the entry of the thugs to rob him and throw him out. The next section, which is longer, because of its added dramatic importance, pursues a similar course again, with the third decoy game this time bringing the entrance of the horrific Mandarin and his dance with the girl. The final section is the chase, culminating in the Mandarin's triumph. Each of these sections, however, can be subdivided, and these divisions bring into account the thematic relationships between the musical ideas. The first section, the Prelude, starts with scurrying string scales and hammered woodwind chords:

If one divides the string scale into two segments, it will be seen that each spans a fourth, the lower one perfect (G–C), the upper one augmented (E–A sharp). The woodwind chord marked *x* also includes these two intervals, dovetailed: a perfect fourth (A sharp–D sharp and an augmented (E–A sharp). This chord is particularly important in the course of the work. Incidentally, the street noises include leaps of a sixth in the brass, written in precisely the same way as in important sections of the later *Sonata for Two Pianos and Percussion*.

When the tumult has died down to a pedal A flat, the vagrants are introduced with an important chromatic motif (Ex 13a). Its brusqueness and jerky nature emphasise its thematic importance, for the derivations of this theme are frequently concerned with the thugs and the girl's association with them, as in Ex. 13b when, with a touch of more painfully heartbroken music, she reluctantly accedes to their demands for her to go to the window:

So in the first section itself we have the two subdivisions: the concert Prelude and then, so to speak, the dramatic Prelude. This latter episode is itself fairly self-contained musically, with its own characteristic themes, as in Ex. 13a and its developments, though obviously it does form part of the scheme set off by the start of the work and is not separated from it. It is closely related to the opening bars, too, especially by the use of rising fourths to accompany the third thug's bullying of the girl to stand at the window.

The second section again subdivides into two. We have, first, the girl's decoy game, signalised by a clarinet theme dominated by fourths and fifths (the latter, of course, being inverted fourths):

The tag at the end should be noted; it is a reminder of the girl's association with the thugs (see Ex. 13a). The girl's dance of enticement here is fairly short, gaining intensity quite rapidly. Eight bars of linking music, a pulsating, crescendo-ing ostinato, in which the timpani play a rhythmic motif in minor thirds, increase the tension to herald the entrance of the elderly rake.

Here the second part of this section begins with grotesque, sarcastic textures, including some of the trombone glissandi which abound in the score. When the rake's 'comic gestures of love' commence, Bartók gives him a pathetic, ironic theme in violas and cellos, both yearning and weird, based, once again, on the interval of a fourth:

As the rake continues to make advances he is given a whining theme on cor anglais, with a lurching accompaniment, vividly conjuring up his wretched state, and as the tension increases with the use of rising themes and tonalities, his melody is given added ugliness in a cello variation.

Then the thugs burst in, to a violent motif that achieves something of the character of a ritornello, and the music disperses itself for the start of the third section. Exactly the same formal process is used here, with the subdivision into (i) the girl's enticement dance and (ii) her dance with the victim. But Bartók varies his basic material considerably. The girl's dance, for instance, is higher in tonality by a minor third, the orchestration is more elaborate (woodwind trills at cadential points, thicker accompanying chords, and the chilly glitter of piano tremolandi as the music progresses), and the intensity is, from the start, greater. The girl's theme itself is changed (compare Ex. 16 with Ex. 14), more decorative and wide-ranging:

This part of the music is also longer, the material more developed, reaching a more decorative climax before the young man is seen, the villains hide and he enters. There is virtually no linking theme this time.

The second part of this section now begins. The shy young man is given a much more relaxedly diatonic theme (on oboe) than any so far in the work, and the predominant interval is again the fourth. As he advances towards the girl and starts to dance, 'shyly at first', he is given a bassoon theme of markedly oriental character in its sinuosity, again full of fourths. 'The dance becomes faster and more passionate', but only briefly, for the thugs rush in to their violent, street-music-like ritornello, and once again the music has prepared itself for the start of a new section.

This time the subdivisions are much more numerous: (i) the girl's dance, once again placed in a higher tonality, with the theme infinitely freer in contour and decorated from the start by chillier elaborations than it has hitherto received (string harmonics, wide-ranging piano arpeggios, and so on), more jagged in outline; (ii) a remarkable passage in which the characters see 'a weird figure in the street', denoted by a pentatonic, viciously harmonised tune in muted trombones and surrounded by hideous orchestral squeals (the vivid similarity towards the end of this passage to some of Stravinsky's *Le Rossignol* must be coincidental), leading to the Mandarin's entrance, signalised by powerful, snarling brass thirds and wild trills on wind and strings; and (iii) with virtually no link as such, but simply a pause on the Mandarin's blaring thirds on the horns, the hesitant start of the girl's dance to the Mandarin.

From here to the end of the Suite the music, having come to a pause before the start of (iii), gradually accumulates the most inexorable tension. At first, as the Mandarin seems to be totally passionless, the girl's dance is tremulous and unwilling; the predominant theme is a sighing, halting waltz theme, and there are frequent pauses, sometimes with chill shudders, before she proceeds further. Gradually, as she tries to elicit a response from the Mandarin, the textures become more elaborate: icy piano, celesta, harp and triangle figuration is added to the increasingly decorative sonorities, the dance becoming wild and ultimately defiant before the Mandarin's thirds blare out once more. The girl resumes her waltz, faster and more frenetic, and then, when she goes to embrace the Mandarin, he begins to 'tremble in feverish excitement' (a passage of astonishing realism).

To link this part of this section with the finale of the Suite, Bartók introduces, against a swirling, frantic background, a trombone theme whose outline, with its exotic nature, foreshadows the forthcoming chase music, and whose trombone colouring recalls the Mandarin's initial presence in the street. The tension is screwed up to breaking point and, against a pounding ostinato, the terrified girl tears herself away from the Mandarin's grasp and the pursuit begins. This is nothing less than a full-blown fugue on a subject the outline of which surely derives from Bartók's Arabian folk-music explorations:

Ex. 17

With entries constantly rising in tonality, Bartók once more increases the tension until the fugue, having reached its peak, breaks up into faster, more brutally blocked textures; his thirds, the chords from his first appearance, and the woodwind chords from the beginning (see Ex. 12) are recalled in harsh brass, while the rest of the orchestra swirls around this material as if trying to tear it to shreds, and the Suite is swept away to its final, catastrophic chords.

The influence of *Le Sacre du Printemps* has been detected in this finale, with its changes of metre and its barbaric ostinato for the fugue. This is arguable, for both elements seem the logical point for Bartók to have reached at this stage in his career in the metrical freedom he had been developing and in the treatment of primitive rhythmic accompaniments in his more festive folk-dances. One recalls the *Allegro barbaro* for piano (1911); the battering rhythmic drive of the Mandarin's fugue is surely a sublimation of the savagery behind this. But the transformation is startling; there is a new bite to the music, and underlying horror that leaves the listener exhilarated but aghast. Motivic development, thematic relationships, dramatic 'illustrations' apart, this is quite simply a terrifying piece of music. To have led up to this degree of tension after so many rises and falls of intensity in the work, and then not merely to have sustained it but to have tightened it still further, is a colossal achievement.

Oddly enough, the Mandarin, for all his repellent aspects and the revolting subject-matter generally, is a more sympathetic figure than Bluebeard, possibly because he is incapable of dying without love, whereas Bluebeard is incapable of living with love. Bartók himself feared that this ballet would never reach the stage because of its story; hence, no doubt, his immediate compilation of the Suite for concert use. With it, he said farewell to the stage; the difficulties he had experienced with his stage ventures, as with his earlier orchestral music, must certainly have contributed towards his reluctance to work further in the medium. Henceforth, much of his activity was devoted specifically to the propagation of folk-music, both pedagogically and in his arrangements, and to the provision of music for himself and his friends to play. Apart from the concertos written for himself or his second wife to play, his remaining orchestral works were all written to commission.

Dance Suite

Bartók said that the happiest days of his life were spent on his folk researches, listening to the music of the people; and his works of the early 1920s vividly evoke the feeling of community and of spontaneous improvisation. The two sonatas for violin and piano (1921 and 1922) are full of this spirit, transformed by the intense nature of Bartók's concert techniques and, for their time, markedly advanced in style, but still clearly derived from this source. So too is the *Dance Suite* for orchestra (1923), commissioned for a concert celebrating the fiftieth anniversary of the unification of Buda and Pest. Like Beethoven in his Second Symphony, Bartók produced in his *Dance Suite* a work of ebullience and delight at a time of considerable emotional upheaval: his mother was experiencing difficulties with the establishment of her nationality following national boundary changes, and Bartók himself was at the time preparing for his divorce from Márta Ziegler and his marriage to Ditta Pásztory. Yet the work is a kind of transfiguration of the ideas behind the earlier *Rumanian Dance* of 1908, formally expanded and infinitely richer in resources. He said that the work showed how much wider his range of folk sources was than that of Kodály (whose masterpiece, the *Psalmus Hungaricus,* received its première at the same concert), without in any way implying any lack of appreciation of Kodály's music, which Bartók always admired. In a letter to Octavian Beu he wrote of the *Suite*:

No. 1 is partially and No. 4 entirely of an Oriental (Arabic) character; the ritornello and No. 2 are of Hungarian character; in No. 3 Hungarian, Rumanian and even Arabic influences alternate; and the theme of No. 5 is so primitive that one can speak only of a primitive peasant character here, and any classification according to nationality must be abandoned.

The rondo-like shape of the chain of dances, with the gentle but pervasive ritornello figure that intervenes between most of the movements, is a typical form, and equally characteristic are the themes themselves, for despite their variety of folk sources they are all original tunes entirely consistent with the stylistic resources Bartók established as his own. There is, clearly, a relationship with the previous ballet score in several respects, not merely the symmetrical arrangement of the ritornello (paralleling both the theme for the thugs rushing in when the girl has decoyed her customers and the use of the clarinet theme with which the girl entices them) but also in the nature of some of the material. The opening bassoon theme, for instance, with its obsessive circling round a few intervals in a close chromatic compass, and its fiercely oriental feeling, recalls the fugue which forms the wilder culmination of the ballet Suite:

This is announced quietly at first, and never achieves anything like the ferocious savagery of the ballet, but it is clearly a member of the same family. Note, incidentally, the effect of the phrasing in the first three bars, for though the notes themselves are the same in each, Bartók achieves a subtle shift of rhythmic emphasis by the different placings for the slur.

Formally, one can say that the *Suite* is a massive expansion of the principles underlying the early piano piece *Evening in the Country*, from the *Ten Easy Pieces*: five sections grouped as three of one type (slow in the piano piece, fast in the *Suite*) interwoven with two of the opposite kind of pace. The addition of the ritornello in the orchestral piece is an extra structural element, providing points of reference to bind the form together and link the dances to each other. The *Suite* actually has six movements, the one labelled no. 5 leading into and acting almost as a Prelude to the Finale (which begins with the rhythmic motif ♩ ♫ which has dominated No. 5). Within each dance, however, the structure is considerably more complex than might seem from the brief description so far given, or from the relaxedly entertaining nature of the music's actual sound.

The first three dances become increasingly complex as they proceed. In the first, the ponderous, twisting bassoon tune and its attendant accompanying figures dominate the movement: there are numerous other ideas, and a certain fragmentation of the material, but we seldom stray far from the opening, though the fluctuations of tempo add to the variety within the piece. There is no major climax; the music reaches a mild peak of intensity and then comes to rest for the lovely ritornello theme to appear in the muted violins. The second phrase is quoted here; the first starts more hesitantly:

This is lightly accompanied by sustained chords, creating an atmosphere of nostalgic pastoral reflection.

With an extension of the ritornello theme, Bartók pauses on a modulatory chord which could go anywhere but which gives way to B flat for the second dance. This is more emphatic than the first, a pounding, primitive piece in which the main theme consists largely of a hammered minor-second interval. There is a clear relationship here with the Scherzo of the Second Quartet, though, as Bartók pointed out, this dance is more Hungarian in flavour. It is more extensive than the first dance, rhythmically more flexible, with bars of 3/8, 5/8 and 7/8 disturbing the essential 2/4 metre of the tune, and also more concentrated thematically; virtually everything in it derives from the minor-third motif. Suddenly the music plunges down to a strong dissonant chord, and on a diminuendo a harp glissando leads to a characteristically altered version of the ritornello, the theme on the clarinet this time and changed in shape, with more inversion.

The third dance commences in a lighter, more cheerful mood. The main theme is more wide-ranging than those of the previous dances, and more openly diatonic, with a subtle hint of bagpipe drone in the accompaniment. It is the most varied of the first three movements in orchestration, with an immense variety of sonority ranging from the glittering to the full-blooded, and it is also the most resourceful thematically, with two important secondary themes. It is in fact a self-contained rondo, with the main theme appearing the second time with vastly different orchestration and the third time with genuine thematic variation as well as a further change in scoring. The spontaneous sound of the dance arises from Bartók's skill in disguising the complexity of the technique; artless it may seem, but it is thoroughly artful.

Without, this time, any hint of the ritornello, and after a general pause (always a dangerous thing to do after what appears to be a triumphant finish, since an audience is liable to think the work concluded), Bartók turns at once to the vastly different world of the fourth movement. This has been likened by several writers to an 'Arabian night', and the pulsating fourth-chords that punctuate the various phrases of the main theme do conjure up most remarkably a sense of a vast, cool desert night. The main theme itself, given first of all to the cor anglais and bass clarinet, winds slowly around itself, languorously and exotically. The structure of the movement is quite straightforward: the theme is divided into phrases, each of which is stated with increasingly rich wind instrumentation, always playing in unison or octaves (there is no counterpoint in this movement at all), until the highest point of richness and expression is reached. Then, phrase by phrase, the scoring is thinned out until the music has returned to the stillness with which it began. Between the phrases of the tune the pulsating background appears, with a kind of inner ritornello function, never reaching the dynamic level reached by the tune but simply providing a setting for it. As the music dies down after the peak, Bartók not only reverses the music (the phrases of the theme appearing in reverse order) but telescopes the events, reducing each phrase of theme and of background to one bar instead of the two-bar phraseology adopted in the first half of the movement. At the close of this hauntingly beautiful piece, there is a reflective reference to a few bars of the ritornello theme in its original shape before the fifth dance, a moderately-paced, pulsating piece, begins.

Here there is virtually no melody as such, simply a rhythmic figure (quoted earlier) and an ornamental twiddle to decorate it. The music gradually piles up fourths one on top of another but hardly increases in dynamics, winding down to the bass again. Suddenly a powerful low brass interjection occurs, to be followed by references to the piled-up fourths and the dance's main motif. It is, however, a short piece altogether, so it is not long before it has wound down to its close: a curiously statuesque, ritualistic piece to be interpolated at this point in the work. But it provides a link between the remoteness of the fourth dance and the unbuttoned vigour of the Finale, which enters without any reference to the ritornello, and once more slowly piles up fourths until all twelve notes of the chromatic scale are throbbing. A variant of Ex. 18 breaks in forcibly, and then a series of brass fanfares based on minor thirds reminds us of the second dance, culminating in a biting emphasis on this interval. Then, with a full-blooded statement of Ex. 18 (the deferred climatic statement from the first movement, as it were), the festivities truly commence. The music whirls along its joyous course, bringing with varying degrees of emphasis tunes from all the previous movements except the fourth; a climax is reached with blazing reiteration of the theme of the second dance.

Here a held dissonance dims into the distance while a harp sweeps softly into the regretful farewell of the ritornello theme. The music picks up pace once again, and several of the work's most prominent themes propel it forward with growing power into the final pages, a strong, apparently final cadence on C and then, after a pause, a brusque cadence on G.

To intrude a personal note at this point, the final cadence seems to me misleading. Bartók has so firmly established a kind of C major just before the end, and so satisfyingly, that it seems somehow inconclusive to cancel this out by changing his mind and coming to rest on a G. But this brings the tonality of the whole work into question, and undoubtedly, subtle though the organisation of this is, G is the work's tonal centre. It is so firmly established at the beginning and end of the first dance that, though most of the movement has other tonal bases, these can be seen only as divergences from the home key. The ritornello, on its first appearance, is initially based firmly on G by its harmonies and the use of a pedal point, despite the tune's B flat major. The second dance is as strongly centred on B flat, but at the end of the ritornello is this time heard above an E flat pedal for its first five bars. In the third dance, with its rondo form, matters are more complicated: the main theme is centred on B on its first two appearances, while in the third it appears in a modal E flat above a C pedal. The two episodes of the rondo shape are basically on G (the first especially, with a drone on G and D running right through it); F sharp (the dominant of B) also plays an important part in the developmental section which separates the first statement from the first episode. Thus, although the third dance is basically in B, this tonality is disrupted by others, of which G makes a significant impression. In the fourth movement, the pulsating background once again centres on G (modal in structure), while the 'Arabic' theme centres on flats (mostly A flat) or sharps. The brief reference at the end to the ritornello states the tune in B flat (with flattened seventh) above an A flat pedal, going down to G in the last couple of bars. This shift from the flattened supertonic (A flat) to G might lead one to expect the fifth dance to start in the work's tonic, which has been thus emphasised. Not a bit of it. Bartók switches to a pedal E which goes almost all the way through this movement, interrupted only by an upward move to G and then back again to E.

The Finale starts with a further move, down to C, and its tonalities are immensely varied. But the music makes significant returns to C (as a drone under a tune in B) and G, which reappears as the pedal note for the B flat ritornello theme. It is interesting that as the work progresses the tonic nature of G should sometimes be strengthened, as in the fourth movement, and sometimes weakened, as in passages where tonal centres such as B and C dominate. G certainly tends to recur at crucial points, but increasingly C makes its presence felt, and one is reminded that if a single note is played for a sufficient number of times, it will turn into its own dominant, and a final fall of a fifth is necessary for a satisfying finish. It is, I suspect, for this reason that I find C the more convincing final note for the work, and this derives from the way Bartók emphasises the essential tonic nature of G, and also suggests towards the end of the work that a fall to C is imminent to round the work off. By accomplishing this, and then reverting to G for a final cadence, he suddenly seems to shift the work's tonal meaning.

The *Dance Suite* is a far more immediately accessible work than *The Miraculous Mandarin*. The tonal orientation just discussed is one reason for this. In the ballet Bartók frequently uses pedal points to give tonal solidity to passages that would otherwise appear to have little or no basic sense of key; and a tonal centre of some kind is always an important functional necessity to him. In the *Dance Suite,* despite the complexity of the music's construction, its more obvious tunefulness and much firmer, more tonal basis give it a more simple appeal. I want to stress its approachability. The details of how the music is built up, and whether or not the last note is the right one, are merely a technical description of the processes that lie behind the music; the essential thing about it is the gaiety, brilliance and vitality of it all. It is small wonder that it was an immediate success, of the kind Bartók had long dreamed of; an exploration of the technical processes behind it merely strengthens one's liking and admiration for what is, after all, a supremely enjoyable work.

After the Dance Suite

Despite the success of the *Dance Suite*, Bartók did not essay another abstract major work for the orchestra until 1936, the *Music for Strings, Percussion and Celesta*. The intervening years, however, saw a crucial period of his career. His growing international fame saw the composition of a wide variety of works. Along with typical groups of short pieces he produced the *Village Scenes* (1924), the Piano Sonata, the suite *Out of Doors* and the First Piano Concerto (all 1926), the Third and Fourth Quartets (1927 and 1928), the *Cantata Profana* (1930), and the Second Piano Concerto (1931), a staggering array of masterpieces. One or two features of these works, though strictly speaking outside the scope of this survey, demand notice in passing. Not the least of their features is the appearance of a characteristic 'night-music' style, which was to become a typically Bartókian slow movement genre, in *Out of Doors*: this movement (*The Night's Music*) evokes the vast Hungarian plain, the impenetrable night filled with the chirping of insects – music of hitherto unique character. In his faster movements of this period, along with the savage, pounding ostinati he uses note-clusters to enhance the primitive, percussive feeling, but in *The Night's Music* the softer clusters and flickering, horizontalised groups disguised as ornamental *gruppetti* give an uncanny effect, impressionistic in a way far removed from the Debussyisms of his early years. It is known that Bartók was influenced by hearing some of Henry Cowell's tone-cluster piano pieces into adopting these techniques; but his way of utilising these resources is entirely his own, and the later orchestral works benefit immeasurably from this widening of his textural 'reservoire'. The First Piano Concerto, indeed, already expands these techniques. Bartók's main rhythmical tunes in this work rely very largely on repeated notes hammered out until they achieve enough power to move away (much as an aircraft revs up until it has sufficient power to leave the ground), and his ostinati frequently involve the use of clusters, while in his orchestration the handling of percussion, always imaginative, grows in resourcefulness; one recalls the slow movement, with its ominous tappings and boomings while the piano steadily builds up an ostinato of six-note clusters in each hand. This was the period of Bartók's most intense exploratory music. In earlier years, his advances had been towards directions other composers had taken: the impressionism of Debussy, for instance, or the expressionism of Schoenberg. Now his explorations turned to an intensification of his own individual aural world, with the result that most of the pieces from this period have taken a long time to reach the general acceptance that is now, in most cases, theirs. Their difficulties, not least for performers, have no longer the aspect of forbidding territory.

The Third and Fourth Quartets mark an intensification not only of Bartók's textural ideas (they are a veritable storehouse of brilliantly conceived sonorities for the medium) but also of his compositional techniques. Here we find an ever-increasing concentration of thought, a fining-down of his cellular techniques, and also two thoroughly characteristic formal organisations. The Third Quartet forms two paired halves: in the first half there is a slow movement and a quick one, and the second half is composed of thoroughly varied reprises of these. The pairing of slow and fast sections on this scale recalls once again the *lassú* and *friss* of folk-music. The symmetrical arrangement of the Fourth Quartet is different: here the central movement of the five is slow, flanked by two lighter pieces – flickering scherzos in this case – which in turn are framed by the weightier outer pieces. Bartók had returned to this five-part scheme intermittently since the *First Suite,* and would do so again.

The tone of these quartets is unremittingly tough, to an extent that makes them still extremely difficult listening – more so, in my opinion, than the quartets of Schoenberg – but in the same period Bartók returned once more to relatively large-scale exploration of folk influences in the two *Rhapsodies* for violin (alternatively, in No. 1, cello) with piano (or orchestra). Possibly his return to these sources for works of moderate size, as opposed to simple miniatures, softened his outlook to some extent; possibly, having in the Third and Fourth Quartets finally achieved the ultimate synthesis of Eastern European folk-music elements and Western concert techniques for which he had so long been striving, he felt more capable of relaxing into more accessible forms without sacrificing his integrity. After the Fourth Quartet his music loses the sense of struggle, of striving after a strong intellectual purpose at the possible expense of subjective emotional feeling, and gradually becomes progressively more communicative, without compromising any of the stylistic integrity for which he has struggled so hard. We can see this in the Second Piano Concerto, written with the utmost rigorousness of technique, employing all the technical poise gained through the experience of the Third and Fourth Quartets, but at the same time possessing a much more accessible expressiveness, at times a joyousness like an echo from the *Dance Suite*. This is not to suggest that the quartets are not masterpieces; they are. But they are as much masterpieces of the composer's innate will to formulate the utmost degree of stylistic synthesis as they are of his ability to write music of immensely concentrated expression. And there are moments, especially in the Fourth Quartet, when the titanic efforts to gain an ultimate indivisibility of style tends to overbalance the expressive qualities of the music and to bring them near to hysteria. Small wonder that having achieved this union, Bartók sought relaxation in the *Rhapsodies,* and hardly surprising that, having achieved the miracle (had he failed, one wonders if he would have been able to write any more), his music from then onwards markedly increased in emotional range.

The Folk-Dances

The orchestral pieces dating from 1931 and 1933, however, have little bearing on Bartók's stylistic development, being arrangements of earlier short piano pieces, rewritten thus solely for the purposes of making money from performances and broadcasts of such accessible works. He had already written works in this folk genre before, once in the *Rumanian Dance* of 1908, and then in 1917 with the *Rumanian Folk-Dances,* a transcription of the piano work written two years earlier and by now, in its various arrangements, possibly his most popular work. The themes are taken from the fiddle-tunes of Transylvania, and the arrangement is predominantly for strings, with solo clarinet and solo piccolo making perfectly judged evocative contributions to two of the numbers, and small wind ensemble adding to the fun in the last two. In the original piano version, and in Székely's familiar violin-and-piano arrangement, the last two movements are a single piece, but in the orchestral transcription Bartók makes clear the separate identities of its two tunes by numbering them separately to make seven dances instead of six. The music is fresh, simple, appealing, and really too well known to need any further comment.

In the *Hungarian Sketches* (sometimes called *Hungarian Pictures*), rather than taking an earlier set and transcribing it straight, Bartók derived a new cycle of pieces from various earlier sources. The movements are:

Evening in the Village: the fifth of the *Ten Easy Pieces* (1908): a tiny rondo-form, and music of heart-easing loveliness and innocence, tinged with nostalgia. (If anything, it is even more affecting in this subtle orchestral setting.)

Bear Dance: the last of the same piano cycle, and thus the first of his Bear Dances: against a fast *ruvido* ostinato the main theme is heard, coloured by whole-tone scale suggestions, and marked orchestrally by appoggiaturas and ponderous comments from tuba and timpani; there is a hint of rondo-form about it, in that the statements of the theme are interspersed with brief 'episodes' in which some of the material is fragmented. There is a delightfully rustic air about the music.

Melody: the second of the *Four Dirges,* probably written in 1909: four statements of a flowing, pentatonic theme that anticipates the opening motif of *Bluebeard's Castle,* with some variation and expansion of the tune, and increasingly lush orchestration.

A Bit Drunk: the second of *Three Burlesques* (1911): Bartók gives a vivid picture, anticipating the more bitter scenes with the wooden puppet and (in the *Mandarin*) the elderly rake, with a tune compounded of rising and falling fourths surrounded by hiccuping appoggiaturas and swaying fluctuations in tempo; the humour is all the more biting in this orchestral version of the piece.

Dance of the Ürög Swineherds: from *For Children* (1908-9): one of the first of Bartók's many dancing, vigorous, cumulatively exciting finales.

This is a thoroughly charming set, requiring only moderately full orchestra, and it is surprising that it does not appear more often as a programme filler. It should be noted that it partakes of one of his favourite symmetrical schemes, with the central slow movement enclosed by two scherzos.

Also dating from 1931, the *Transylvanian Dances* are a straightforward arrangement of the Piano Sonatina of 1915, the melodies of which are once more derived from the Transylvanian district of Hungary, with its predominantly Rumanian style of folk-music. In the orchestral version one is made even more aware than in the original of the skill with which Bartók evokes the rustic atmosphere. In the first movement, *Bagpipers,* the first and third sections of this ternary-form piece are exceptionally onomatopoeic, while the lighter middle section is more dance-like in feeling. The second movement is another *Bear Dance,* with a rich, ponderous string tune simply played through twice, with changes in the accompanying harmonies and a slow lightening of texture; there is little of the grotesquerie of the *Bear Dance* of the *Hungarian Sketches.* The finale, the most extended movement, though only two minutes long, contains two tunes, both lively, the first accompanied by a drone D and the second freer in harmony. Two years later, in 1933, Bartók made a further transcription of similar kind, the *Hungarian Peasant Songs,* derived from the piano pieces of the same name written in 1914–18. The opening section, *Ballade,* is a theme and variations starkly presenting the tragic story behind the folk song with only slight polyphonic treatment. The style of the remaining pieces is akin to that of the *Hungarian Folk-Dances,* i.e. simply harmonised arrangements of folk-tunes rather than, as in the *Transylvanian Dances,* some small degree of development or formalisation.

Music for Strings, Percussion and Celesta

Bartók returned to full-scale abstract orchestral composition only in 1936 with the *Music for Strings, Percussion and Celesta.* He had meanwhile produced his Fifth Quartet, an especially significant work in that, while not a whit less concentrated in thought or technique than its predecessors, it is a good deal more expressively expansive. The process by which Bartók was now able to reveal the full extent of his expression had begun. In the *Music for Strings* we see this clearly. It was commissioned by Paul Sacher for his Basle Chamber Orchestra, and it adopts the typical scheme of two pairs of contrasted movements. In some respects it is the consummation, among his orchestral works, of several trends he had been pursuing, notably the use of single notes as tonal centres rather than fixed keys (there is a distinct relationship with Hindemith's handling of tonality in this respect), the unity that Bartók finds between apparently utterly disparate styles (intense chromaticism cheek by jowl with clear diatonicism, without any incongruity), and above all the thematic unity achieved by close interrelationships, an aspect of his technique that in this case makes use of a motto theme, rather than simply a motivic element, running through the whole work. There is also his handling of the spatial aspect of the music, with two string orchestras separated by the percussion, an aspect deriving to some extent from the increasingly blocked-out orchestration in the *Dance Suite* and from the first two piano concertos, treated here with immense cunning in the development of the material.

The first movement is perhaps the most remarkable in the work. It is an astonishing flow of sustained music, progressing from the dark of A to the light of E flat (a tritone away) and back again to the dark of A – Bartók's beloved arch form. This is achieved by the longest, most intense fugue of his career. It is, in fact, an unbroken stream of notes producing a compelling, gripping, hypnotic power. Even in the quartets, which this movement more closely resembles in concentration than any other movement in his orchestral works, there is no single span of music so limitless in feeling or continuous in nature. But at the end of the movement, when most composers would be content to rest on their laurels and turn to some new material, Bartók has by no means finished with his fugue subject – it dominates the first movement to the exclusion of counter-subject, and it pervades the remainder of the work – Ex. 20 overleaf.

In order the excerpts in Ex. 20 are: the fugue subject of the first movement, the main theme of the second movement, the opening viola theme of the third, and, from the finale, the first subject and then the diatonicised transformation of (a) that forms the high point of this movement. But virtually every theme or movement in the whole composition is derived from Ex. 20a; to quote any more would not, I think, illustrate the work's inner unity more than these do.

From this fugue subject itself three features should be particularly noted: the two marked in Ex. 20 with square brackets, both motifs of special importance to the work, and the rising minor third

formed by the two notes marked *x*. These are elements from which the entire work is largely made, thematically, by a process as rigorous as any in the quartets. What makes it so remarkable a composition, however, is not merely its intellectual concentration of thought, formidable though this is, but the whole world of experience gained through its pages. It is music of universal passion, however apparently intellectual its formation. In the third movement, too, Bartók displays a new ability to harness his immense textural resources, in this instance his 'night music' variety, to the expression of a new emotional force, which is far from being merely an exercise in fascinating sonorities. Together, instrumental colour and motivic technique form an indivisible unit.

The meaning of music is essentially a personal matter, but it may be relevant to refer for a moment to the third movement's emotional significance. Bartók's own view of life derived largely from a deep love of nature, and, one feels, a deep suspicion of man, at any rate sophisticated man (in which it is easy to sympathise with him). The disruptions in his later slow movements are very often caused by the intrusion of a 'human' emotionalism into music profoundly expressive of natural beauty or spaciousness. In this third movement, only the anguished, tragically uncertain but highly emotive viola theme (Ex. 20c) disturbs the remote feeling behind the music. The rest of it, however intense, retains a sense of inhuman iciness that sets the human elements into focus. Formally, especially according to Bartók's already established habits, this movement demands a fast developmental follow-up, but emotionally one feels one would like to go away and not be disturbed for a while, to think about the implications of this haunting music. Its extraordinary, chilly involvement makes one sorry that the finale sweeps in with a boisterous folk-dance atmosphere that is delightful, but which seems somehow vaguely irrelevant. After a couple of pages the listener is swept along irresistibly, but the regret initially affects my own reaction, at any rate, to the opening of the finale.

This is not intended, however, as a criticism of Bartók's composition, merely as a comment on the depth of feeling which the third movement draws upon; and certainly the finale, from a structural point of view, makes a supremely satisfying ending to the work as a whole. In this connection one might recall the Third Piano Concerto, his last completed piece. This is much more relaxed in tone and has often been accused, along with the *Concerto for Orchestra,* of being an attempt to make his music 'easier' for the listener in an endeavour to reach his public more quickly; in other words, a relaxation of his high ideals and therefore a pandering to the masses. This view is still, to some extent, held by those unable to reconcile the concept of music that reaches out towards its audience with the ideal of stylistic integrity. It is still held to be true, in some quarters, that to be of any value music must be 'difficult' and certainly not popular, though nowadays the opposite view is also maintained by those who think that for music to be valid it must be as determinedly popular as possible – which usually involves an inbuilt element of manufacture in order to appeal to the largest possible audience. When one comes to look at the Third Concerto, it is a moving and beautiful work in which the profoundly simple slow movement, far from being simplistic in order to be 'accessible', is a deeply felt expression of the composer's essential spirituality, while the finale emerges quite naturally, with apparently spontaneous exuberance. There is no sense of momentary evasion of the issues raised by the slow movement when the finale starts; the miracle is that the dying man could write music imbued with so deep a sense of peace and optimism. It is in the finale of the *Music for Strings* that Bartók, now a complete master of all his techniques, is able to take the first steps on the road towards this final optimism, for the section in this movement which resolves my own personal doubts about it, and forms possibly the high point of the entire work, is the introduction of Ex. 20e, the more diatonic version of the all-important motto theme. At this point Bartók picks up the problems of the *Adagio* once again and resolves them, affirming an essential human nobility and warmth. It is, so to speak, a final answer to Bluebeard's isolation. It can be no coincidence that Bartók's future works should increase the range of this warmth, so that the Sixth Quartet, for all its tragedy, should be the most supremely expressive of the set, nor that the bitterness or sadness expressed in his remaining works should always be of a more directly communicative kind, more immediately emotional in its humanity than the equivalent sections of works during the preceding decades.

Curiously enough, the first movement of *Music for Strings* is at once one of the most intensely anguished pieces in his output and one of the most powerfully communicative so far. Technically it is a highly systematic fugue, the entries of the subject being alternately higher and lower by a perfect fifth each time (upwards: (A)-E-B-F♯; downwards: (A)-D-G-C); after the central climax on E flat the subject is inverted and, from the start of the celesta arpeggios which so subtly radiate the textures, presented in both original and inverted forms together, the last phrase of the movement spreading outwards and then inwards again in both directions from a unison A and back again, a summary of the process underlying the movement as a whole. Yet despite the extreme concentration and working-out of technique, the feeling is of immense passion, starting with numb, isolated grief, growing almost imperceptibly at first, but with increasing power, to the central impassioned climax, and then returning to the opening mood, given an added cold glitter by the celesta's figuration. This last is a typical example of Bartók's use of colour to enhance the emotional depth of the music; the cymbal roll just before the climax is another superb touch, widening the emotional horizons and preparing us for the intensity of the climactic E flat. The technique, however involved and refined, is utterly subordinate to the expressive needs it serves.

The second movement is a brilliant, vitally rhythmic dance movement in an expanded sonata form. The main theme (Ex. 20b) has elements of the first movement's fugue subject both in the circling nature of bars 6–8, with the upward movement from a C and then a return to the same note with a certain amount of chromatic elaboration of this basic idea, and also in the rising minor thirds, thrice repeated, with which this *Allegro* starts, clearly derived from the motif *x* in Ex. 20a. The development section is extensive, including a fully-fledged fugue on a tune which, by basing itself on bars 6 and 7 of Ex. 20b but concentrating it within a smaller intervallic compass, clearly reveals the relationship of this theme to the motto theme. The recapitulation is at first metrically uneven, but becomes predominantly 3/8 in metre, a further example of Bartók's habit of changing some aspect of the material even when he appears to be repeating it more or less strictly.

The brilliant forward drive of the second movement carries us away from the taut emotional grief of the first, with no sense of incongruity or lessening of intellectual fervour. When the *Adagio* appears we are somehow ready for the issues it raises; only when, following this, the finale enters is there any jarring of the work's intelligible and logical emotional progress. This is despite the clear relationship of the main theme, Ex. 20d, to the motto theme, whose rise and fall is now inverted; the new diatonicism of the theme introduces what sounds like a totally new element into the proceedings. The contrasts have hitherto been part of the work's progression; now the sudden change of mood twists the work in a new direction. Only when it becomes more frenetic in the passage leading up to the expanded, warmer version of the motto theme (Ex. 20e) does it all fall into place. Here the questions of the *Adagio* are answered positively. At the triumphant end of the work the finale is retrospectively seen as an utterly logical culmination. It is a miraculous achievement to have dared for so long the dangers of seeming to evade the *Adagio's* implications before finally resolving them, and only the supreme, concentrated nature of Bartók's thematic technique enables him to bring it off.

The feeling of the finale is rondo-like though, as in the *Dance*

Suite, it is more a garland of ebullient folk-dances closely interrelated and gathering up the threads of the whole work towards the end, with a new depth of meaning. The third movement, however, is an extraordinary form (one should note, incidentally, how each movement of the work presents a different, *echt* Bartók structure, built with the utmost thoroughness). It is a kind of expansion, or variation, of his beloved five-part shape in which the central part is framed by pairs, like ripples in a pond. Here the centre has been shifted to the fourth of six sections, thus:

A B C D C/B A

The arch-form this represents, with the suggestion of a palindrome, is strengthened by the fact that during section D the music actually turns back on itself and starts to move backwards. While not strictly adhering to this palindromic technique, Bartók observes its general outlines in reversing the order of events, so that the music ends up where it began, with a xylophone tapping a written-out *ritardando* (instead of a written-out *accelerando* as at the start). He compresses his 'reversed recapitulation', however, by combining in the fifth section the high, keening violin theme (a close variant of Ex. 20a) from section B with the celesta, harp and piano figuration from section C; and the last section of all is a much shorter version of the first, in effect only a brief reminder of it. In a sense one might even call this an extreme variation of sonata form with the exposition reversed to form the recapitulation, and section D as the development; but D is hardly conventional as such. It is, rather, an increase in intensity, based on a five-note motif which gradually gains in pace and dynamics, only to exhaust its own momentum before the 'recapitulation' commences. It is a curiously stark, almost brutal passage marked by the striding, percussive treatment of its motif, and by placing it at the height of the movement Bartók emphasises its inhuman coldness of impact. To be thoroughly fanciful, it is for all the world like the inexorable march forward of Wells's visitors from Mars. It is precisely this inhuman element and the contrast with the few touches of frozen humanity in the viola tune (20c) and the high violin theme mentioned just now that give this movement its gripping but awesome impact. This is far removed from the isolated but immensely passionate outcry of the first movement; the sense of relief achieved by the transformation of the motto theme at the peak of the finale is tremendous.

Divertimento for Strings

There is none of this frightening remoteness about the *Diverti-mento,* though here, too, Bartók gives us a slow movement of great power. It was written in 1939 in the short space of three weeks at Sacher's chalet at Saanen, in the Swiss Gruyère massif. Sacher, who commissioned the *Divertimento,* enabled Bartók to escape from the turmoil of the world around him, which broke out into the Second World War; and after completing this work Bartók immediately plunged into the Sixth Quartet. The more valedictory, elegiac nature of the quartet can be explained not only by the more intimate nature of the medium, in which Bartók could communicate with absolute directness his innermost feelings about the world, but also by the news of his mother's death, which reached him while writing it. His reaction to humanity's behaviour in general also explains the bitter acidity of the quartet's humour. In the *Divertimento,* however, only the tragic slow movement shows his deep concern and fear for humanity; in the outer movements he produces the most relaxedly entertaining and easily assimilated music he had achieved in his major orchestral output. Yet there is no sense of incongruity: if the peasants are dancing under the shadow of an immense catastrophe, the tragedy is all too human, unlike the extraordinary spreading of inhuman wings expressed in the *Adagio* of the *Music for Strings.*

The orchestral technique of the *Divertimento* emphasises Bartók's classicism; if the *Music for Strings* is his equivalent of Beethoven's C sharp minor Quartet, this is his concerto grosso, with its use of solo instruments to form a concerto group against the ripieno background. He does not employ this technique systematically or self-consciously but quite spontaneously, yet his manner of doing so vividly calls to mind the world of the concerto grosso. The dance-like nature of the two fast movements also reminds one of the dance-form basis of the Bachian suite. The apparently unforced gaiety of the outer movements hides a wealth of thoroughgoing motivic development, in typically Bartókian fashion. In the first movement, in which the extrovert spirit of *verbunkos* is meta-morphosed into a powerfully pulsating symphonic dance, the main theme, firmly in F major but with a flattened seventh pushing it forward almost from the start, and with strong suggestions of

B natural (Lydian mode) in the accompanying harmonies to broaden the tonal horizons further, is infectiously flowing:

The movement is in sonata form, though a thoroughly Haydn-esque one, with the recapitulation so strongly permeated by a varia-tion of its material that it seems to be a further development section. Furthermore, the second subject and its subsidiary material are both heavily influenced by little scalic motifs derived from the main theme, so that the music achieves a close unity that the variety of tempi, textures and tonalities can never dispel. Even though the coda is a tranquil reflection on the main theme, there is sufficient motivic strength in the first movement to enable it to lead, quite naturally, into the darker world of the slow movement.

In this *Molto adagio* we are plunged into a funereal world, reaching its peak in the third of the four sections. In the first a winding, cellular theme is heard on second violins (Ex. 22), a motif – it is hardly more – that has obvious potentialities for thematic expansion (seen already at work in the third and fourth bars) and variational development:

Under this theme there is a constant flow of slow, semitonal quavers, creating a vague restlessness which is to some extent dispelled by the more openly diatonic nature of a theme based largely on fourths and heard on the first violins. This brings a slight suggestion of consolatory warmth, soon dispersed. Suddenly a unison D, a cry from the upper strings, cuts through the textures and heralds the second section. The main motif of this (Ex. 23) is a sobbing lament from the violas:

It reaches a climax, only for the music once again to die down to a pause. With an almost medieval bareness, a deep pentatonic ostinato harmonised in open fifths and fourths begins in the lower strings, to which are added slowly rising violin trills, consistently cut off; the music becomes more and more anguished as the trills rise to their peak, only to die down slowly to a series of pauses interspersed with reminders of the central catastrophe. The music returns to the opening material, with shuddering tremolandi colouring the flowing quaver accompaniment and more varied handling of the initial motif of Ex. 22, and the movement gradually winds to a still ending on an open *major* third (a hint of consolation to come?) after one final violin outcry.

After this intense, shattering expression of tragedy and lamenting, so human in its feeling, the finale brings a complete change of mood – yet the sweet major third at the end of the *Molto adagio* has implied some possibility of redemption. It is a complex rondo form, complex because some of the episodes are closely related to the opening theme (Ex. 24), while some of the returns of the rondo theme are themselves variations of it:

Ex. 24
Allegro assai
[Violin 1]

It is prefaced by a few bars of introduction starting on a strong G and a partly chromatic scale upwards, landing on a powerful chord which could go to any one of several keys. Having had his little joke, Bartók settles for F major (though, as Ex. 24 shows, as strongly influenced by the flattened seventh as Ex. 21 was) and the rondo is cheerfully under way. Two particular sections are of special interest structurally. One is the fugato that forms, at any rate from the aural point of view, the centre of the movement. This is in effect one of the ritornello sections, but it is based on a theme which is a distinct variation of the main theme:

Ex. 25
(♩ = 96–100)

The falling fourths at the start of this, the falling fifth (bars 5–6) and its rhythmic style clearly relate to Ex. 24, though it sounds very much like a new theme. It is stated by the strings in unison and then developed in a double fugato, in which a counter-subject is present throughout. This is short-lived, however; the strings then announce, in unison, an inverted version of Ex. 25, and a new fugato starts with this as its subject. Its progress is soon halted by a reduction in pace and dynamics for a passage in which first the solo cello and then the solo violin rhapsodise on derivations of the same tune. The violin, indeed, develops a small cadenza, having started by freely distorting the melody. A little imitative phrase based on the last two bars of Ex. 25 brings the music to a pause, as if looking round for the right road, and then the movement regains its poise and spirit, once more to sweep forward. The fierce humour of this strange section is expressed in terms of acute formal balance within the context of the move-ment as a whole.

So too is the process of increasing wildness and then fragmenta-tion which leads to the other significant episode, even more odd in appearance. This is shortly before the end, and once again it is for all the world as if the music had got out of control and capsized before Bartók picks it up off the floor, winds it up, and sets it in motion again. It is signalised here by the introduction of a *schmaltz*y pseudo-Viennese polka, quite slow, clearly related to the main theme, with the violins playing pizzicato, the cellos and basses plucking their polka accompaniment, and the violas commenting with a couple of wry glissandi. But this brief episode, one of the rare excursions in the orchestral music into Bartók's vein of slightly perverse wit (though by no means as grotesque as the five-finger exercise interrupting the Fifth Quartet's finale), is soon over, and the work whirls away to its scintillating finish.

Concerto for Orchestra

The story of Bartók's emigration to the USA and his struggles with both ill-health and poverty is well known and needs no re-telling here. But it is worth pointing out that things were not completely desperate; despite his worries for the future, his leukaemia (eventually to kill him), and his concern for humanity, he had influential friends in the USA, among them Szigeti. He it was who had already been instrumental in persuading Benny Goodman to commission *Contrasts*, and it was he who, with other friends, prompted Koussevitsky to commission the *Concerto for Orchestra*. The commission had to be offered discreetly to avoid any suggestion of charity, which would have offended Bartók's pride; even so, Koussevitsky had great difficulty persuading the sick composer to accept the advance fee. But the stimulus provided by the commission enabled Bartók to break the virtual silence he had observed since his arrival in the USA, for since the Sixth Quartet he had composed only two works, both transcriptions of earlier pieces intended for himself and his wife to play at their concerts: the *Concerto for Two Pianos and Percussion* (a version of the *Sonata for Two Pianos and Percussion*) and, in 1941, the *Suite for Two Pianos* (from the *Second Suite*, for which he retained, obviously and justifiably, a strong affection). But now Koussevitsky's offer fired his imagination, and he produced his first new work for some time. It was to be an instant success, even more so than the *Dance Suite* of twenty years earlier, and it marks a further stage in the increasing accessibility of his music after the Fourth Quartet.

This new approachability is, as already suggested, not a sudden unfurrowing of the brow but a logical culmination of the expressive trend of his music over the past decade. One can see the final works as the culmination of this progress, with the serenity of the Third Piano Concerto marking a radiant close to his output.[1] In the years between the Sixth Quartet and the *Concerto for Orchestra* the creative silence was surely due to causes not dissimilar to those causing the much longer hiatus in Rachmaninov's output, including heartsick nostalgia for his native land. (I often wonder how those who accuse Bartók's last works as being a weakening of his ideals account for the 'popular' and relaxed style of the outer movements of the *Divertimento*.)

The *Concerto* has three notable aspects, which Bartók himself avowed. He called the work 'symphony-like', and indeed it is a genuinely symphonic composition, the sublimation of the large-

[1] The Viola Concerto is purposely omitted from these remarks; Serly completed it from Bartók's often confused sketches, and so, remarkable and moving though it is, it stands outside the context of his completed œuvre.

scale unity he had attempted in his early years without having the technique to achieve it in the way necessary to him. A conventional symphony by Bartók is, somehow, unthinkable; the nearest he got to one was in the two early Suites and the unsatisfactory *Four Pieces*, Op. 12. But this *Concerto* represents the aims of these works, conceived on a grander scale and accomplished with absolute mastery. Bartók admitted that the use of this particular title was due to the virtuosic nature of the orchestral writing, in which virtually every player becomes a soloist. There is also a mild programme behind the work, which he outlined thus:

The general mood of the work represents, apart from the jesting second move-ment, a gradual transition from the sternness of the first movement and the lugubrious death-song of the third to the life-assertion of the finale.

This is an apt summing-up of the impression the work leaves, but it naturally cannot convey the richness of invention, the abounding technical resourcefulness, or the sheer verve and vitality of the music.

As in so many of his earlier works, the arrangement of the movements is five-part: the central slow movement (*Elegia*) flanked by two pieces of lighter texture (*Giuoco delle coppie* and *Intermezzo interrotto* respectively), these in turn framed by move-ments of greater structural weight. This symmetrical scheme is enhanced by the fact that the pace of the movements increases outwards from the centre, so that the third movement is the slowest, the second and fourth are, basically, somewhat quicker, and the first and last are, again basically, the fastest. The two lighter movements, moreover, though relaxations of the work's intensity, are immensely striking in themselves, and their basic ideas and working-out are so characterful and strongly expressed that they in no way represent any lessening of the work's total impact. But the relaxed tone of the *Concerto* as a whole, and its immediately entertaining nature, can easily mislead one into taking it for granted; the organisation of the material is exceptionally complex, more involved and varied even than in the *Music for Strings*. A close study of the score will reveal, in almost every bar, some typical Bartók devices. At the very beginning, for instance, the pentatonic preludial figure on cellos and basses is followed by a soft string shimmering that sounds merely impressionistic, but

in fact spreads out from a C to a major third on either side of it
(C – D – E upwards, C – B♭ – A♭ downwards) and then returns
to C via the notes omitted before (E♭ – D♭ and A – B), a systematic exploration of a group of four semitones up and four
semitones down, amounting in all to a horizontalised tone-cluster,
from A flat to E natural. And, of course, one notes that the upper
line is inverted to form the lower line, the two heard jointly. The
stuttering flute figure which follows ends in contrary-motion
scales, as if vanishing into the distance, an enchanting 'night music'
effect under the spell of which one can easily miss the thematic
implications of the scales, the upper one a simple chromatic and
the lower one similar save for the omission of one note and therefore an extension of the scale by a semitone. At the second
repetition of this process, some of the material is already beginning
to be developed – the bass theme is extended, and the flute phrase
goes outwards in a more circuitous fashion. And this only in the
first page of the score, in a texture which seems to be a simple
but evocative scene-setting!

Thus it is that the technical devices Bartók now has at his
command are made to serve his expressive needs to such an extent
that their complex nature is almost completely disguised. Even
when one is aware of some fairly obvious motivic development,
the recognition is almost subconscious; the emotional effect is
what strikes home. For instance, in the *Intermezzo interrotto* the
charming, folk-like opening theme is recalled after development
on the cor anglais. The effect is one of simple charm, touching
nostalgia, and possibly something even more profound than these;
one is aware of the thematic aspect without really noticing it, so
artless is the effect of this example of Bartók's constant delight in
thematic variation. This movement, though, demands closer
attention, for it contains several elements which are equally
striking, not least for their emotive suggestions.

It commences with a fragile, hauntingly lovely oboe theme, folk-
like in feeling and strongly coloured by the presence of the tritone.
Having pursued its course, with some fragmentation and development, Bartók then introduces a more luscious melody, reminiscent
of a popular Hungarian art-song of the period between the wars,
'Hungary, gracious and fair'. There is something profoundly touching in Bartók's handling of these two themes, as if he were giving

expression to his homesickness not in anguish but in a spirit of nostalgic acceptance. The delicate profundity of the music is emphasised by the brutality and coarseness of the notorious Shostakovich episode which breaks into this atmosphere. As the tempo quickens, the clarinet introduces that infamous theme from Shostakovich's *Leningrad Symphony* representing the Nazi invaders, which Bartók heard on the radio during this time. He decided to express his contempt for what is surely the worst theme Shostakovich ever wrote, and the effect of this is quite shattering. Howls of laughter from the woodwind, rude noises from the lower brass, and then a viciously swirling circus background throw the violins' attempt to make the theme respectable into a contemptuous light; it does not sound distinguished even when put upside down – indeed, it sounds even more ludicrous. A final squeal from the woodwind, dispersing the merriment (hollow laughter at best), and then, with heart-rending poignancy, Bartók brings back not the first theme from the earlier, lyrical section, but the lusher second, with its overt Hungarian associations. The first theme reappears a few bars later.

The emotional effect of this odd sequence of events is most disturbing. To all intents and purposes the two lyrical themes are charming, slightly sad and rather delicate. But the Shostakovich episode gives them, both in retrospect and on their reappearance, an added depth; the movement becomes a bitter comment on life and its disruption. If this is wit, it is wit of the most profound psychological penetration. Together with the *Elegia*, which is, so to speak, the less bitter, more impassionedly emotional side of his nostalgia (largely taken up with a powerfully anguished, haltingly Magyar-flavoured tune accompanied by richly funereal throbs), these two movements form the core of the work; for I feel that the *Intermezzo interrotto* is as personal an expression of feeling as the *Elegia*, couched in terms far more elusive because apparently humorous. In all this, it would be easy to miss the fact that the *Intermezzo* follows its own five-part symmetrical scheme: ABCBA, the C being the Shostakovich passage.

It is striking that genuine wit appears only in the orchestral works of Bartók's last decade. The relaxation and expansion of his expressive world enables him to explore many kinds of wit in this period, from the savagely expressive nature of the *Intermezzo inter-*

rotto or the *Burletta* of the Sixth Quartet (which casts a strong shadow over at least one theme in the *Concerto's* finale) to the light-hearted humour of the outer movements of the *Divertimento*, especially the last. But the second movement of the *Concerto*, the *Giuoco delle coppie* (*Play of the couples*), is an utterly unique inspiration of the most delightful wit, worked out with a thoroughness belied by the surface lightness of touch. After a preliminary, relatively unemphatic call to order on the side-drum (unsnared) the bassoons enter with a theme that can be described as a faintly solemn but slightly ridiculous swaggering,[1] for all the world like two clergy-men trying to appear dignified after having consumed one glass too many of vintage port:

Ex. 26

The impression of slight inebriation held under control is en-hanced by their attempts to reach a top note, successful only at the third attempt (bars 5–9). The form of the movement is ABA, with A as a series of variations on this theme and B devoted to a simple chorale theme in the brass (one is reminded here of the serenely beautiful chorale in the slow movement of the Third Piano Concerto). It is an altogether charming and delectable movement, but once again its superficial accessibility can easily lead one to overlook the rigorous methods employed in handling the material, mostly achieved by scoring, and above all by the handling of the pairs of instruments rather than by extensive thematic transformation. Each pair of instruments without imi-tative counterpoint or canonic devices performs the main theme in parallel at different intervals, to enhance the character displayed by each statement of the theme. The bassoons are in sixths, digni-fied and vaguely pompous (one would normally never dream of

[1] This needs the most acute judgement of tempo if its essential character is to be properly realised; John Pritchard, in his Classics for Pleasure recording (CFP 176), does this to perfection.

describing the interval of a sixth as pompous, but it is so here). Then the oboes have the tune in minor thirds; both the instrumental colouring and the choice of interval give it a faintly clucking feeling – perhaps the clergymen's housekeepers have emerged, after a little too much sherry in the kitchen? The clarinets, in sevenths, then provide the theme with an added touch of rubato and a new, slightly whining air. The flutes, in open fifths, add a flavour of warmer lyricism to the proceedings, extending the theme and decorating it. But muted trumpets, in seconds, view the tune (and the clergymen) with something approaching malevolent sarcasm, and the side-drum calls this part of the movement to a halt and leads to the chorale.

In the return of section A, the bassoons, oboes, trumpets and clarinets mostly retain their characteristic intervals for the theme, only the flutes being changed (to sevenths). There is a good deal of variation, with a new counter-subject (on a third, rather more sprightly bassoon) and some combination of pairs of instruments (clarinets and flutes play together, making up chords of superimposed fourths with their dovetailed sevenths, the oboes and clarinets playing together with the latter inverting the theme of the former). The serene poise with which all this is accomplished is utterly miraculous; it is a lovable, ridiculous piece.

I have dealt at some length with what appears to be the least important movements of this work precisely because they are the ones most easily taken for granted – the *Giuoco delle coppie* especially, since though one is instinctively aware of the devices that are used to make it, it is so purely diverting that one's analytical faculties are disarmed. In the outer movements the music is more obviously complex and tightly integrated, so if one is going to explore Bartók's subtle techniques in this work these are where one is likely to do so. They represent, in my view, the summit of his achievement as a composer of large-scale music; the thematic interrelationships are worked with a stunning economy of means and with an equally stunning richness of imagination along lines already developed throughout his career. It is a summation of his life's work, and there is no better assessment of it than the remarks of Halsey Stevens:

If it is eclectic to combine oils, pigments and canvas from recognised sources into an original and personal work of art, then this is an eclectic work and

Bartók an eclectic composer. . . . But the identification of the raw materials of a work of art neither condemns nor exalts it. Its content and its significance depend upon more fundamental considerations. If the creator has something trenchant to say, and says it with the greatest sincerity of which he is capable, microscopic dissection is pointless. Bartók's *Concerto for Orchestra* is a great work, one of the greatest produced in this century, not because of the startling originality of its materials or the novelty of their treatment, but because the problems it poses are broad and vital ones, solved with the utmost logic and conviction.[1]

[1] In *The Life and Music of Béla Bartók* (New York & Oxford, revised ed., 1964).

Index